Quilt Note

Trapunto originated as a decorative quilting technique. Samples of this type of needlework date back to the early 1400s.

Traditionally, the designs were stitched with white thread on white fabric. The patterns were easily seen at close range, but were nearly invisible from a few feet away. Because Donna wanted her work to be enjoyed from a distance, she experimented with colored thread for the stitching and a darker colored thread as the filler in the channel. This combination of colored thread and colored yarn creates a readily visible trapunto design.

The finished appearance of the work is determined by the use of a variety of threads and the color intensity of the yarn.

Trapunto is one of the most simple and relaxing forms of needlework. It is portable so it can travel with you to appointments and other events that require waiting. No hoops, charts, counting threads or extra equipment are required.

Choose a design, gather a few required materials and begin the fun of exploring trapunto.

Meet the Designer
Donna Friebertshauser

Donna Friebertshauser's love of needlework, art and dimensional crafts have influenced this book. She is an art professor specializing in needlework and fiber-art classes at Coastline and other community colleges in southern California. The requests of her Exploring Needlework students for additional and original trapunto designs influenced her to expand her three self-published books on the subject into *All About Trapunto*.

Donna's designs and articles featuring a variety of needle techniques have been published in needlework and craft magazines and books. Her designs and kits have been included in various needlework catalogs and as a Book-Of-The-Month selection.

She has taught at local, regional, national and professional seminars, as well as on a cruise to Alaska.

Donna has co-authored and judged the Counted Thread Master Craftsman program for the Embroiderer's Guild of America. In 2003 she received a Distinguished Service Award from Coastline College's department of visual and performing arts.

Donna is owner of Crafts By Donna, a mail-order business specializing in kits and supplies for Battenburg lace, Brazilian (dimensional) embroidery and other needle techniques.

In addition to needlework, Donna enjoys gardening, learning new craft and needlework techniques and experimenting with new materials and designs.

Trapunto Basics

Trapunto is used to raise the surface of a stitched design. Methods or styles include corded, padded, appliquéd-and-padded and blackwork. Designs are transferred to a top fabric, a second layer of fabric is basted together with the marked top and the design is outlined with stitches. The channel or space created by the stitches is stuffed from the back side to create the raised surface. The results vary with the chosen method.

BASIC TOOLS & SUPPLIES

There are a few basic tools and supplies common to all types of trapunto. The following list includes everything you need to stitch a sample and guides for their selection and use.

Fabric
Types of Fabric

Two layers of fabric are needed for all trapunto—a top fabric on which the design is marked and a lightweight back fabric. The back fabric should not show through on the top fabric. For appliquéd-and-padded trapunto, patterned fabrics may be used because the design areas in the fabric may be padded. Fiber contents may vary.

For corded trapunto to show color, the top layer of fabric should be a solid-colored light-to-medium weight fabric such as batiste, symphony, polyester broadcloth, etc. To prevent affecting

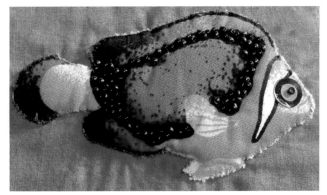

the top fabric color, use the same-color fabric for both the top and the back.

The top fabric for padded trapunto is frequently a preprinted polyester broadcloth, drapery fabric, etc. Choose a print that has one or more design sections that can be emphasized or made dimensional by padding. Solid-color muslin or broadcloth is used for the bottom.

Aida 14-count is used for blackwork trapunto. An Aida thread is actually made with many single strands but is counted as one thread. Do not split the threads when stitching.

Fabric Preparation

Wash, dry and iron all fabrics before starting a project. Washing removes excess sizing so the stitching is easier and takes care of any shrinkage before stitching. (See Blackwork Trapunto on page 14 for information on Aida-cloth preparation.)

To stabilize the edges of both top and back layers of fabric, use a temporary hem. This may be machine serging, zigzagging or overcasting by hand. Do not use a liquid stabilizer, tape or glue.

Select the best fabrics you can afford with a high thread count and close weave.

Lightweight Iron-On Interfacing

For appliquéd-and-padded trapunto, a lightweight iron-on interfacing is used to stabilize the fabrics.

Interfacing is used when you want to cut appliqué shapes without the bother of adding seam allowances and turning fabric edges under. The interfacing acts as a stabilizer on the edges.

Before cutting out the design, apply the lightweight iron-on interfacing to the wrong side of the fabric, referring to the manufacturer's instructions. Cut the design area exactly to size, avoiding a seam allowance altogether.

To avoid raveling, handle the pieces as little as possible during the stitching process.

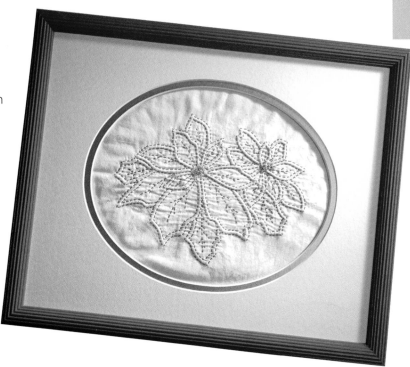

Thread

Today needleworkers have a large variety of thread choices. You might want to experiment with a variety of types of thread before choosing the one that works best for you.

Threads should be colorfast. If they aren't, the color will run onto the background during the rinsing process and remove pattern markings. See Bleeding Colors on page 9 for more information.

Types of Thread

Spun threads are those with individual fibers that are spun into single strands that are then twisted together; cotton or polyester threads are examples of spun threads.

Core threads include a core strand of polyester that is wrapped with a spun cotton or spun polyester.

Multiple strands of either rayon, polyester or nylon are twisted together to form 1 strand of filament thread. Rayon is the weakest of the filament threads and usually not colorfast. Nylon melts easily and may get brittle and discolor over time. Polyester is the most popular type of filament thread.

Monofilament is a single strand of nylon or polyester thread. When invisible stitching is required, monofilament may be used.

Specialty Threads

There are many other specialty threads such as metallic, silk, pearl cotton, etc. These threads may be used to add a different dimension to the stitching or add embellishments to your stitched design.

Embroidery Floss

Embroidery floss may be cotton, rayon or silk. Cotton floss is made of 100 percent long-staple mercerized cotton with 6 strands twisted together to form one thread. Solid colors work best for trapunto stitching, but variegated creates a nice look. Dye lots vary, so be sure to purchase enough of a color to complete your project.

Rayon floss gives a sheen to trapunto stitches, similar to the look of silk but at a lower cost. Silk is more expensive and less durable than rayon, but if using silk fabric for the stitching base, it is better to use silk floss for the stitching.

Metallic embroidery floss is available in multiple strands and adds a different dimension to stitching. Select this type of floss to add a sparkle to a project.

Using Embroidery Floss

I recommend using 1 or 2 strands of any type of floss for trapunto stitching. Because the needle wears on the floss as it is pulled through the layers, move the needle closer to the thread ends as you stitch to avoid having the needle in the same place on the strands for every stitch.

To use, pull a 15" length of floss from a skein. Separate the 6 strands into separate strands by pulling 1 strand straight out while holding the others. Stitches are made with 1 or 2 strands of floss. Keep the strands separated for all stitching; do not allow them to twist as you work.

It is easier to thread a needle with 2 strands of floss if you treat them as 1 strand by folding the floss ends over the end of the needle and pinching them together while pulling them off the end of the needle. This tightened loop is easy to thread through a needle's eye. A needle threader is also helpful

Yarn

Yarn is inserted in the channels in corded, machine and blackwork trapunto. Purchase 4-ply knitting worsted weight.

For corded and machine trapunto, select a color to match or coordinate with the color of the thread or floss used to stitch the channel lines of the pattern.

Fiberfill

Fiberfill is a fluffy polyester or Dacron stuffing used to add dimension to padded trapunto or appliquéd-and-padded trapunto. It is hypoallergenic and washable.

It is inserted through openings left in seams and through slits cut in the back fabric.

Needles

There are several types and many sizes of hand- and machine-sewing needles. Several different sizes are

used in each type of trapunto. If you have a problem pulling a needle through your fabric, especially when using yarn in corded trapunto, use a small piece of a balloon, rubber jar opener or fingers from rubber gloves to provide a good grip on the needle.

Types & Sizes

Sharps are needles with a sharp point and are used to pierce the fabric. Crewel, embroidery and straw (milliner's) are examples of sharp needles.

Tapestry needles have rounded points which allow them to pass between fabric threads. These are used for cross-stitch, blackwork and hardanger embroidery and for inserting yarn into the channels of corded trapunto. A No. 22 needle works well for this.

Use a sharp-pointed needle for basting and stitching the trapunto designs. A No. 7 embroidery needle has a slender shank but an eye large enough to easily thread.

To add beads and other embellishments to the designs, use a No. 10 beading or embroidery needle.

Needle Storage

Keep needles in the closed, tarnish-preventative pack in which they were sold. If you don't have that, store in a piece of wool or wool batting. Needles will rust, so never leave one parked in your project. If this happens, it is hard to remove and leaves permanent rust marks on the fabric. Needles may rust when left in a pin cushion for long periods of time as well.

Tip

A reason for storing needles in the purchased package is that it is easy to identify the type and size of the needle when selecting one for a particular use.

MARKING SUPPLIES

Transferring patterns to fabric requires marking tools. These marks should not be visible on the completed project. There are several methods and products that aid in this very important step of the process. Actual marking and removing marks will be discussed in detail in the Transferring the Design to Fabric section.

Water-Erasable Pen

A water-erasable pen is a commercial marking pen that makes marks that disappear from fabric when immersed in water. It is easy to trace designs onto fabric with this type of marker. Do not substitute air-erasable markers because the design disappears from the fabric after a few hours.

Sample showing marking with water-erasable pen.

Solvy water-soluble film can be purchased from Sulky at www.sulky.com.

Sample showing marking with water-soluble film.

Water-Soluble Film

Water-soluble film is a slightly opaque film used to transfer designs to fabric. The design is drawn onto the film with a permanent black ink pen. When stitching is complete, the film and ink lines are dissolved away with cold water. Sulky manufactures the product, Solvy, that may be used for this process.

Water-soluble film packets can be purchased from Donna Friebertshauser at designsbydf@aol.com

OTHER TOOLS & SUPPLIES

There are many helpful tools and supplies that a stitcher can use to help make things easier. Thimbles, sharp scissors and shears, and common pins, preferably with large heads, are among the basics. There are few specialty tools that really aid in the process.

Needle Threader

Trying to get a piece of 4-ply yarn through the eye of a No. 22 tapestry needle can be quite a challenge. If you don't have a commercial needle threader, you can make one of your own.

Cut a piece of paper (typing or other similar weight) about 1" long and the width of the eye. Fold the paper in half to form a V (Figure 1). Insert one end of the yarn directly into the V. Fold the paper down on top of the yarn. Put the paper and yarn through the eye of the needle. The single thickness of yarn will easily go through the eye.

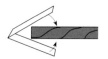

Figure 1
Fold the paper, inserting yarn into the folded V.

This type of threader is also excellent to use when working with multiple strands of cotton floss, metallics or any combination of thread and yarn.

Hoops

Hoops are two rings of either wood or plastic that fit together and hold the fabric taut for hand embroidery. For machine embroidery, look for a thin hoop that will fit under the presser foot of the machine. To avoid stretching, remove either type of hoop whenever the sample is not being stitched.

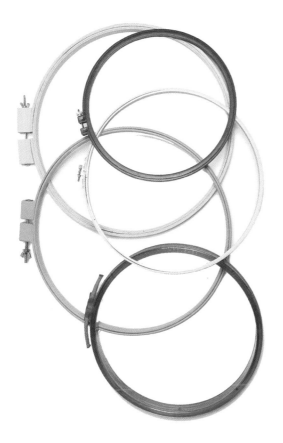

Beeswax

Beeswax is produced by many species of bees. A stitcher passes sewing threads over the wax to lubricate the thread. This makes it easier for the thread to slide through fabrics and reduces the wear on the thread. Do not use beeswax on stranded cotton embroidery floss.

Stuffing Tools

A stuffing tool is a long slender tool that is required for padded trapunto and appliqué-and-padded trapunto. It is used to poke the fiberfill into the areas to be padded. A sanded bamboo stick, such as a chop stick, knitting needle, small sanded dowel, mechanical pencil without lead, stylet or other pointed object may be used. Do not use the points of scissors or shears, a sharpened pencil or any sharp object that might pierce or mark the fabrics.

TRAPUNTO TECHNIQUES

The trapunto techniques covered in this book include corded trapunto, padded trapunto, appliqué-and-padded trapunto and blackwork trapunto. The patterns given in the pattern section of this book may be used for any one of these types, but are best suited for corded and blackwork trapunto.

Each type of trapunto is covered here, and some project examples are shown.

Many of the techniques or instructions apply to more than one type of trapunto. These techniques are given here as general information. Refer to this section often for specifics on these basic methods.

Transferring the Design to Fabric

Wash your hands before you begin; do not use hand lotion after washing.

Once fabric has been selected and prepared and the pattern has been chosen, the design has to be transferred to the fabric. The design lines are the guides for stitching but are not permanent and must be removed when stitching is complete. There are two basic methods that help make this an easy process.

Using A Light Source

If you are fortunate enough to have a light table, even a small one, you should have no problem transferring a design to fabric. You may use other methods if a light table is not available. If it is bright outside, one of the easiest methods is to tape the pattern to a window, and place the top piece of fabric over the pattern and trace the design onto the fabric.

Make a light table using things on hand. Use an old window or a piece of glass. Tape all edges of the glass to prevent cuts. Open a table that allows the insertion of a leaf, place the glass over the opening, position a lamp beneath the glass and you have a homemade light table. A glass-topped coffee table works perfectly if you don't want to build one and you don't mind sitting on the floor when transferring your designs.

If the design is visible through the top fabric and does not require a light table, place a piece of white paper under the pattern and begin to trace using a water-erasable pen. If your hand is shaky and the line skitters a little, don't worry. You can correct minor errors as you stitch. The blue ink lines will be removed when all stitching has been completed.

Water-Soluble Film

An alternate method of transferring the design to the fabric is using a water-soluble film such as Solvy. This film is opaque enough that the design may easily be copied without the use of a window or a light box.

Simply place the film over the design with the smooth side up and trace using a permanent black pen such as a fine or ultra-fine Sharpie. Do not use this pen directly on the fabrics as it is permanent.

Special Marking Instructions

Some designs have channels that pass over and under other channels—mazes and interlocking designs are examples. Care must be taken that the ends of both channels are not completely closed. The resulting enclosed section would be impossible to later fill with yarn (Figures 2 and 3).

Figure 2
This drawing shows incorrect stitching at intersection channels.

Figure 3
This drawing shows correct stitching of intersection channels.

To define the top or crossing channel, I put extra ink lines in that section as the design is traced. These lines will be removed later, so there is no need to worry about how heavy they are.

Basting the Layers Together

Once the design has been transferred to the top fabric, it is necessary to baste it together with the backing fabric. This may seem like a waste of time, but the final appearance of the completed project is worth the extra work.

If water-soluble film is being used, place the smooth, marked side up on the top fabric. Pin both fabric and film layers together.

Basting should be done with a sharp needle and a light-color sewing thread that slightly contrasts with the color of the top fabric. Use long basting stitches to make removal easier.

Tip
Avoid a dark-color thread, as it might leave a trace of color on the fabric when it is removed.

Begin basting at the center of the project and stitch toward the corners and outside edges of the fabric (Figure 4).

HOUSE OF WHITE BIRCHES, BERNE, INDIANA 46711   WWW.WHITEBIRCHES.COM

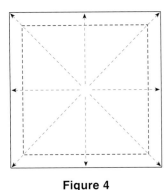

Figure 4
Baste as shown.

Tip
Do not baste from corner to corner or side to side. That tends to push the fabric ahead of the needle and distort the fabric.

Baste around the edges of the fabric. If the design is large or the fabric is slippery, it may be necessary to baste around the edges twice.

Removing Marked Lines or Film
When stitching is complete, pattern markings or water-soluble film must be removed.

Tips
Before removing the temporary design lines or water-soluble film, compare your work with the master pattern to be sure all of the design has been stitched. Sometimes the marked lines make it difficult to see if all areas are completely stitched. This is especially true if you are stitching with a blue thread that is close in shade to the blue color used in the marker. It is easy to check on the back fabric to determine if the entire design has been stitched.

Immerse the entire piece in cold water (without soap or detergent). The ink/film should disappear in a few seconds. Rinse several more times even when the lines/film are no longer visible. Never iron or apply heat to the fabric if any of the ink remains. The heat may set the color permanently.

Tip
Some stitchers try to remove the blue lines with a wet cotton swab or cosmetic ball; this does not completely remove all of the marking pen's residue resulting in a blue halo or shadowing on the fabric.

Bleeding Colors
The secret of preventing or minimizing thread colors from bleeding is to remove all of the water as fast as possible and to dry flat.

If some dye is visible after the cold water treatment, try one of the following remedies: Place the fabric in warm water with a non-bleach detergent recommended for colors. Allow the work to soak for a few minutes. If any color remains, repeat this process with fresh warm water and detergent. Or, soak the work in Biz, an enzyme-based agent. This non-chlorine bleach should not affect your work.

Once the unwanted color has been removed, rinse the piece several times in water. The final rinse water should be free of all detergent. Use distilled water for the final rinse to avoid the possibility of any mineral in the water causing spots or discoloration over the years.

DRYING
Remove the fabric from the water; do not wring or squeeze as the resulting creases may be difficult to remove even when the fabric is ironed.

Place the wet fabric flat on a dry towel and roll up; do not hang wet/damp needlework. It usually takes more than one dry towel to get all of the moisture out. Hand-smooth out the wrinkles as much as possible while the fabric is in this wet/damp condition and laying flat. You may press the fabric dry provided all of the ink/film has been removed. Remove all basting stitches. ■

Corded Trapunto

The most common method/style of trapunto is corded. It consists of two parallel rows of stitching to create a channel. Yarn is then threaded through the channel to create a raised, colored surface.

Check out Corded Trapunto in a Nutshell (page 13) for photo examples of the step-by-step process for creating a corded-trapunto design.

Refer to the Trapunto Basics section for fabric choice, tools and supplies needed and transferring and removing the design from the fabrics. The following instructions add to the general information specifically for corded trapunto.

Choosing Thread Color

Select thread, floss or specialty threads referring to Basic Tools & Supplies in Trapunto Basics. Choose yarn or similar cord to be inserted inside the channels between the two layers of fabric. The density of the top fabric will greatly affect the final color of the yarn. A very bright, vibrant-color yarn will often appear as a soft muted color.

To determine the color of the stitching thread, place the yarn between the top and bottom fabric. Place several potential threads on the top fabric next to the section of chosen yarn. Choose a darker shade in the same color family as the yarn color for the stitching thread. The use of a darker stitching thread intensifies the color of the finished piece.

Stitching the Design
Getting Started

Most trapunto projects are worked without an embroidery hoop. Use a sharp needle and the chosen thread. The stitched designs in this book were stitched with 1 or 2 strands of cotton floss, 1 strand of EdMar Glory, 1 strand EdMar Iris or 1 strand of DMC rayon floss.

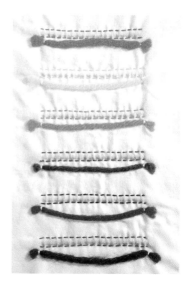

This yarn chart sample shows how the yarn color matches with the thread/floss used to create the design. Notice how the color changes once it is inserted inside the channel. It appears much lighter than the bright color of the yarn alone.

A short running stitch is used for all stitching (Figure 1). This stitch is similar to the one used for basting except the length is shortened. More than one stitch may be put on the needle before pulling it through the fabric.

Figure 1
Running stitch.

Some stitchers make the top stitch slightly longer than the bite into the fabric. This allows more thread color to show. Other stitchers prefer the top stitch to be the same size as the bite. Practice both methods to find the one that is comfortable for you. No matter which method you prefer, keep the stitch length or spacing between stitches consistent throughout the entire piece.

Begin stitching in the center of the design and work out toward the edges.

Corded trapunto consists of two parallel rows of stitching, called a channel. The rows are approximately ⅛" apart, **Note:** *The stitches of the channels do not have to be opposite each other as shown in Figure 2.*

Figure 2
Stitches on opposite sides of the channel do not have to align.

Begin stitching with a secure knot in the end of a 15" length of thread. The use of a knotted thread is contrary to most types of needlework but is necessary for trapunto. When ending a thread, secure the end with a backstitch or double stitch on the back fabric and inside a channel. **Note:** *These backstitches will be concealed when the yarn is inserted in the channel.*

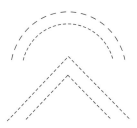

Stitching Curved, Pointed & Intersecting Channels

Most of the designs in this book have curved and/or pointed areas (Figure 3). It may be necessary to slightly shorten the running stitches on the inner section of a curve or slightly lengthen the stitches on the outside of a curve.

Figure 3
Curved or pointed stitching.

Tip

Recall how a marching band executes turning corners. The pivotal person on the inside marches in place while the other members on that line take slightly longer steps to make the curve. Repeat this same procedure in stitches.

When a design has a pointed section, stitch right to the tip of the point. When a channel passes under another channel, stitch up to the edge of the crossing intersection. Plunge the needle to the back and come up on the other side of the top channel. Since the channels are so narrow, the small amount of thread on the back will not be a problem.

Important Note

Every time you are stitching and come to a basting thread, cut and remove that small section of thread. Never stitch over a basting thread. The removal of this small section of thread eliminates the possibility of permanently catching some of the basting thread in your stitching.

Filling the Channels With Yarn

After the channel lines are stitched, remove design marks, dry and remove basting before preparing to fill the channels with yarn.

Inserting the Yarn

Thread a No. 22 tapestry needle (rounded point) with a single strand of worsted-type yarn. Use any length of yarn, but 12"–15" is a good length. Shorter pieces may be used if the area to be filled is small. Do not knot the end of the yarn.

A point is filled by having the yarn/needle go to the very tip of the point before bringing the needle out and back as shown in Figure 6. Failure to go to the tip of a point will result in a design area with no yarn color on the front of the project.

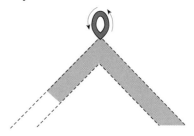

Figure 6
To fill a point, bring the needle out and back at the very tip of the point.

Ending or Adding A Piece of Yarn

When it is necessary to work with another piece of yarn, simply bring the threaded needle out of the channel on the back. Leave a tail of about ¼". If additional yarn is required in the same channel, insert the needle with a new piece of yarn in the same hole. Leave an unknotted tail and continue filling the channel.

When all of the channels have been filled with yarn, you may want to trim the tails and/or large loops on the back to an approximate ¼" length. Do not cut the yarn too short.

Begin working anywhere on the design. Work from the back or wrong side of the project. Insert the yarn-filled tapestry needle through the back fabric only and inside a channel. Constantly check that the needle has not accidentally gone through the top fabric.

Leave an unknotted yarn tail of approximately ¼"–½". Slide the needle along the channel as far as you can without distorting the fabric. When the needle can go no farther pull the needle/yarn out of the back fabric as shown in Figure 4. Leave a small loop—just enough to go over the tapestry needle or approximately ⅛". Insert the needle, back into the very same hole and continue filling the channel.

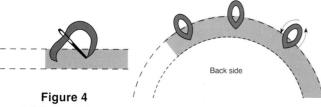

Figure 4
Pull the needle/yarn to the backside.

Back side

Figure 5
To fill a curved section, come out on the back, leave a loop and go back into the same hole; repeat along curve.

Filling a curved section of a design requires that you come out, leave a loop and go back into the same hole. Repeat this multiple times along the curve as shown in Figure 5. The rigidity of a steel needle will not allow pulling yarn around a curve in one movement. It is better to make several of these stops to be certain that the entire curve is filled with yarn.

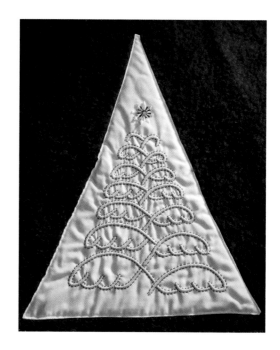

Why Have the Tails?

The little extra yarn loops on the back allow for possible shrinkage or distortion of the design. This is especially necessary if trapunto is being used for clothing or any items that will be moved or manipulated.

Your trapunto project is now complete and ready to be finished in any manner you wish. Do not press your completed trapunto piece. The yarn in the channels creates a dimensional effect; an iron will destroy this. ■

Tip

Traditionally, there were no tails on the back of the trapunto work. Instead, the stitcher carefully pushed aside, on the back, all the fabric threads in the center of a channel. The yarn was inserted in the channel and the small hole carefully closed. The back was smooth with no yarn, tails, etc. showing.

TRAPUNTO IN A NUTSHELL

Photo 1

Begin with a marked design and fabric layers basted together as shown. A dark-color thread was used in the sample so that it could easily be identified. Do not use a dark-color thread for basting in your projects.

Photo 2

The design has been stitched and the marked lines and basting have been removed.

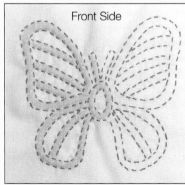

Photo 3

Half of the design has been filled with yarn. Notice how visible the knots are on the back side, and that they are not visible on the front.

Photo 4

Finished stitched design.

Blackwork Trapunto

BLACKWORK STITCHING

Blackwork is a counted-thread embroidery technique. Straight stitches are worked on an even-weave fabric (Aida) or needlework linen.

> **Tip**
>
> As early as the 14th century, blackwork embroidery was a popular form of needlework in Spain. Those geometric designs are reminiscent of popular Moorish architecture.

Black silk thread stitched on white linen or fine fabric was the traditional embroidery technique. Frequently, pure gold threads were included in the design. Today's stitchers are following traditional patterns, but using colored threads and still calling it blackwork.

Originally this embroidery had to be reversible since both sides of the fabric were visible. In order to achieve this reversibility, the double running stitch was used. This stitch is worked with a tapestry needle by stitching every other thread on one trip around the design. After completing this trip around, you have to come back and fill in the open spaces (Figure 1). This creates a reversible line of stitching with even amounts of thread on both the front and back of the fabric. On the return trip, some needleworkers prefer to change from the tapestry needle to a sharp needle. This allows the returning needle to pierce the existing decorative thread in the next hole.

Figure 1
Stitch every other thread on 1 trip around the design and then go back and fill in the open spaces.

It is best to use a hoop or frame to hold the fabric taut while stitching. An embroidery stand or clamps to hold the hoop or frame allows you to stitch with two hands. Place your dominant hand under the fabric to receive the needle. The other hand pushes the needle straight down through the fabric. The dominant hand (on the back) pushes the needle straight up to the top. This will seem very awkward at first, but don't give up. Once you begin stitching this way, it will become easier, and the resulting stitching will look more consistent and neat.

          HOUSE OF WHITE BIRCHES, BERNE, INDIANA 46711   WWW.WHITEBIRCHES.COM

This method of stitching is frequently called "up-and-down", "punch-poke" or "stab" stitching. The latter method sometimes results in some of the Aida holes being enlarged if you are not careful.

A backstitch is also commonly used, though it is not reversible. There is more thread on the back of the fabric than on the front. The tapestry needle comes up at point 1 and down at point 2, advances to point 3 and comes up, and then down at point 4 (Figure 2). The needle comes up on the odd numbers and down on the even numbers. The down needle will share a hole with the adjacent up stitch except for the very first stitch.

Figure 2
The order of stitching is shown for a backstitch.

With either the double running stitch or backstitch, keep the line of stitching smooth on the front (Figure 3). Only the back of the work will reveal which stitch was used.

Figure 3
The line of stitching should be smooth and in a straight line.

BLACKWORK TRAPUNTO

Blackwork trapunto is similar to blackwork embroidery except that the two lines of stitching for the design create channels that are filled as for corded trapunto. The work does not have to be reversible, so a backstitch may be used.

Not all quilt patterns may be adapted to accommodate channels for receiving the yarn filler like the pattern given, but you might like to experiment with your favorite quilt patterns.

Getting Started

You will need an even-weave fabric, such as Aida cloth, for the top fabric and a same-color solid fabric for the back. Gather the basic tools and supplies and prepare the fabrics for stitching, referring to Trapunto Basics. Use a tapesty needle No. 22, 24 or 26 (size depends on what you can thread) and a sharp crewel-embroidery needle. You also need a hoop smaller than the Aida cloth, and cord or yarn to fill the channels.

You may use thread to contrast with the Aida cloth including embroidery floss, pearl cotton or other thread.

Blackwork designs are usually printed as a chart. This means it is not necessary to mark the design on the Aida. One square on the chart equals one thread of Aida. When reading the chart, count the threads and not the holes. The design given is very easy and doesn't require a charted pattern. The number of spaces to count between lines of stitching are given instead.

If you are not familiar with Aida, carefully look at the fabric. There are a number of threads woven together to form a small square. That square is counted and called one thread. Do not split the square.

Baste the Aida and bottom fabric together. If you plan to use the double running stitch, place the basted fabrics in a frame using thumbtacks or staples, making sure the Aida threads are horizontal and vertical before tigntening stitches.

To keep the framed Aida clean as you work, tack a piece of muslin, cotton or any type of fabric around the outer edge of the frame. Your hands will touch this fabric instead of the Aida. When the blackwork stitching is complete and removed from the frame, this waste fabric may be discarded.

Thread for Blackwork

Refer to Trapunto Basics for thread suggestions. The outline on the sample was worked with 2 strands of floss (separated and put back together). If you want a bolder or darker design, use more strands of floss in the needle.

Beginning to Stitch

Stitch all of the outline sections using your choice of stitch and weight of thread. Keep the line of stitching smooth and even.

Once the outline channels have been stitched, you have two choices. You may fill the channels with yarn as described for corded trapunto and leave the interior sections plain as shown in the sample project, or you may stitch a design in each open area. If you plan to stitch designs, do so before filling the channels with yarn.

Use one less strand for stitching these designs than used for the channel stitching to create the look of light and dark areas.

The numbers at the bottom of each section of the Whirligig pattern given in Figure 4 refer to the placement of the numbered stitches. Count 28 squares on the Aida between sections of the design as shown. Leave three squares open in each channel to allow for yarn to be inserted. When stitching is completed, insert yarn to fill channels referring to Corded Trapunto on page 11. ■

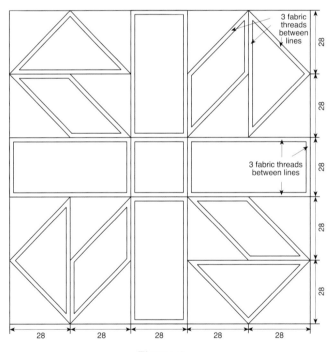

Figure 4
Use the numbers on this design to count
squares to create the design on Aida.

Trapunto by Machine

If you prefer sewing by machine rather than by hand, you will be happy to know that the corded and padded forms of trapunto may be done with a sewing machine. Most of the required supplies will be the same as for the hand-stitched versions.

Getting Started
Gather basic supplies and tools as listed in Trapunto Basics.

Two pieces of fabric are also required for machine trapunto. Select thread and yarn as desired for project. Prepare fabric and transfer the design to the fabric as for corded trapunto. Machine-baste the layers together, if you prefer.

You might think that using a double needle would create the perfect channels for stitching, but I have found that this results in too much thread on the back, making it almost impossible to insert the yarn into the channel. Instead, use a single needle and stitch two parallel lines using the edge of the presser foot to keep the distance between the lines consistent.

Machine Stitching
Depending on your machine-sewing skills, you may opt for the use of a hoop to help hold the two fabric layers together even though they have already been basted. Use a flat hoop with a spring action commonly used for machine embroidery.

The length of the stitch is a personal choice. I prefer the stitches to be fairly close together to emphasize the thread color.

All designs have one or more of the following stitching components: straight lines, curves, points, crossovers, etc. A long stitch may not be practical for some of the designs. Therefore, vary the stitch length and consistency to fit each pattern.

Begin working at the center of the design and stitch to one end of one channel. A second parallel line stitched ⅛"–¼" from the first stitched line will complete a channel. Repeat from the center to the opposite side; do not reverse stitching at the beginning or end unless the end goes off the fabric completely. Instead, leave 1½" thread ends at the beginning and end of the stitching to be secured later.

For a channel passing under another channel, stitch to the intersection, lift the presser foot and pull the fabric from the needle so that approximately 1½" lengths of top and bobbin threads are free of the fabric. Cross the upper channel, put the needle down on the other side of the crossing channel and continue stitching. The "Never stitch over a basting thread" rule also applies to machine stitching.

When all of the stitching has been completed, and before removing the drawn pattern lines, secure the 1½" loops or ends of thread. Cut each loop in the center, resulting in a ¾" length of each thread. Pull the top threads to the back of the fabric. Tie each top thread with the matching bobbin thread on the back. Repeat with other thread ends. This step may seem unnecessary, but if the threads are not tied at each intersection, the channels may partially unravel when the yarn is inserted.

Removing Marked Lines
Before removing any of the lines drawn on the top fabric, compare the stitching with the master pattern. Be sure all lines are completely stitched. Check on the back side of the design as it is easier to see any unstitched areas.

Refer to Trapunto Basics for washing out the marked lines or removing water-soluble film. Refer to Corded Trapunto to insert yarn into channels. ∎

Padded Trapunto

Some historians refer to padded trapunto as boutis needlework. This is a raised-and-stuffed embroidery technique thought to have originated in Sicily during the 13th century.

Padded trapunto is quite different from corded trapunto. It does not have a design defined by stitched channels. Instead, designs may be drawn on a solid fabric and stuffed with fiberfill or designs in a printed fabric may be the focus of the stuffing. Appliquéd pieces may also be substituted for the printed designs. The combination of printed-and-appliquéd sections can produce unique and beautiful projects.

When a solid-color top fabric is used, the design is defined by stitching with a thread that matches or contrasts with the fabric color. Either choice results in beautiful needlework. The basic techniques for padded trapunto will apply whether the top fabric is printed, appliquéd or outline-stitched.

For all padded projects, the design is outlined with small stitches. Tiny slits are cut in the back or bottom fabric within the design area. Fiberfill is added to fill the area between the top and bottom fabrics. Be careful not to put too much padding in the area. The slit is then stitched closed.

What You Need to Get Started

For your first project, choose a fabric for the top layer that has a preprinted design you would like to enhance. It is easier to begin with medium-to-large shapes rather than tiny ones. A heavier-weight fabric may be used than that used for corded trapunto. Appliquéd shapes may also be stuffed (see Appliquéd-&-Padded Trapunto on page 19).

The backing fabric is cut the same size as the top fabric. Use a solid-color fabric rather than a print that might detract from the designs on the top fabric. The bottom fabric may be a lighter-weight fabric than the top.

Collect basic tools and supplies as listed in Trapunto Basics including a sharp crewel, embroidery or milliner's needle, fiberfill, other basic tools and supplies and a stuffing tool. Embellishments are optional.

Stitching

Prepare fabrics for stitching referring to Trapunto Basics.

Stitch around the entire portion of the design to be padded or elevated. Check that the stitching is close together and completely outlines the design. On busy prints, it is easy to skip an area. Skipped areas will affect the placement and smoothness of the fiberfill.

There are two ways to insert the fiberfill into an outlined shape. Both methods are worked from the back piece of fabric.

In the first method, the fabric threads may be

moved aside to form an opening where the padding may be inserted. After the padding is complete, the fabric threads are moved back into place. The back is completely smooth with no visible indication to show where the padding was inserted.

In the second method, a small slit is cut in the center of the design area in the back fabric, being careful not to cut the top fabric. Small pieces of the fiberfill are inserted into the cavity using a stuffing tool to get the fiberfill into all of the curves and points.

As you fill the design, check the appearance on the front. Keep the fiberfill fluffy and evenly distributed. Do not stuff too tightly or the stitching threads will be strained, and the fabric will become distorted.

Close the slit with small overcast stitching using thread that matches the color of the bottom fabric to keep the back of the work neat. There is a tendency to pull when the slit is closed. This tension usually causes puckering on the back. Keep the back as flat and smooth as possible. ■

Appliquéd & Padded Trapunto

The term appliqué comes from the French word appliquér, which means to "put on." Appliquéd-and-padded trapunto refers to complete or partial designs, cut from one or more fabrics, that are stitched to a background fabric and then padded or stuffed with fiberfill.

A stitcher may choose to use a design element in the fabric, such as a printed flower or fish, or use a pattern to cut these same shapes from fabric. With either choice, or a combination of both, a stitcher can mix-and-match many design elements to create a new design as shown in the Aquarium Jewels and Beacon of Light projects.

The appliquéd pieces may be lightly or heavily padded. When an appliqué shape will not be heavily padded, it may be easier to embroider or embellish it before cutting it out. In this case, the design is traced onto the fabric with a water-erasable pen, and embellishments are added or embroidery is stitched within the traced lines before cutting out the shape. Because the embellishments may reduce the size of the design area, check the design size again after stitching and before cutting to be sure it is still the size required and adjust as necessary.

If you plan to use the decorative stitch or embellishments to compress the fiberfill to emphasize a design or shape, add them after the shapes have been appliquéd in place.

Most appliqués should have no raw edges. One method is to turn under a very small seam allowance of ⅛"–¼" on all sides of the shapes. When cutting out the appliqué shapes, be sure to allow extra fabric all around for this seam allowance.

A turned-under seam allowance results in two layers of fabric to be appliquéd. Curved edges require special treatment. A convex curve has too much fabric to turn under; cut and remove small notches of fabric along the curve (Figure 1). A concave shape requires slashes on the inside of the curve (Figure 2). For either type of curve, be very careful not to snip the fabric beyond the seam allowance.

Figure 1
Cut and remove notches of fabric in convex curves.

Figure 2
Cut small slashes in the seam allowance of concave curves.

If a double thickness of fabric is too bulky to turn a smooth curve, there is another method for attaching appliqué. Referring to the manufacturer's instructions, apply a lightweight iron-on interfacing on the wrong side of the fabric before cutting out the design. Be sure the interfacing completely covers the design area to be cut and removed. Cut the design area exactly to size, avoiding a seam allowance altogether.

Before You Begin
Once a pattern has been chosen, select the fabrics based on the design. For appliqué, that might mean many different fabrics including solids or prints. Purchase a lightweight iron-on interfacing to back lightweight fabrics to keep underneath fabrics from showing through.

Refer to Trapunto Basics to collect basic tools and supplies, including fiberfill for the stuffing and crewel or embroidery needles.

Appliqué Placement
Spread the top fabric out on a flat surface. Begin to place the cut-out appliqués in various locations to see what design appeals to you. If you are using an appliqué with a seam allowance, turn it under and securely baste the seam allowance in place.

Arrange the appliqués in desired positions on the top background fabric; pin and baste each appliqué in place.

Place the basted top over the back fabric. Pin and baste the top and bottom fabrics together.

Stitching
There are two ways to attach an appliqué. I prefer to blindstitch each piece in place. This uses a stitch that is not easily seen or noticed. Once the appliqué is firmly attached, you can place a decorative stitch to cover the seam.

You may also use only decorative stitches for attachment. Although these stitches add to the appearance of the finished project, they may not securely attach the appliqué to the background fabric, especially when the appliqué is later padded with fiberfill. If decorative stitches are desired, add after the appliqués are sewn in place.

HOUSE OF WHITE BIRCHES, BERNE, INDIANA 46711   WWW.WHITEBIRCHES.COM

Padding the Appliqué

Once the appliqués are firmly sewn in place, it is time to pad them. The amount of fiberfill used will be determined by how much dimension is desired.

Pad each appliqué in the same manner as for padded trapunto. When cutting the small slit on the back, cut through both the back and top fabrics, but not the appliqué.

Carefully insert pieces of the fiberfill under the appliqué. Do not push too hard or put strain on the appliqué stitches. Check the front design to determine the correct amount of padding. Do not overstuff the appliqué. When the design is padded as desired, stitch the slit on the back closed.

Embellishing an Appliqué

You may embellish an appliqué design before stitching it to the background or after. If the appliqué will be only slightly padded, the

embroidery or beads may be added to the shape before stitching to the background. It is easier to work with the small shape rather than the larger background.

If the beads and/or embroidery are being used to sculpt the designs, then applying them after attaching the appliqué to the fabric is a must. This is an excellent way to give depth to certain areas, e.g., flower/leaf veins, faces, body parts, etc. To vary the amount of sculpting desired, put more fiberfill in some areas than others or, increase the tension on the sewing thread to pull a bead deeper into the fiberfill beneath.

Any time you use beads for embellishment or for sculpting a design, select a good-quality sewing thread and a No. 10 embroidery or beading needle.

Knot the thread and come up from the back to the front of the design. Go through the bead from left to right and down to the back just on the other side of the bead (Figure 3). Next come up right next to where you went down, pass through the bead from right to left and down to the back (Figure 4). This crossed stitch will pull the bead upright so the side color of the bead and not the hole of the bead shows. Continue to stitch other beads, carrying the thread from one bead to the next. Use this same method to attach all types of beads including seed, bugle and ornamental.

Figure 3
Begin by stitching
left to right.

Figure 4
Finish by sewing
right to left.

Backstitch under each bead to lock it in place and ensure that if a thread should break in the future, you will lose one bead instead of many. ■

Daffodil

HOUSE OF WHITE BIRCHES, BERNE, INDIANA 46711   WWW.WHITEBIRCHES.COM

Flowers in the Round

Rose
Sew a small pearl to petal to represent a dewdrop.

HOUSE OF WHITE BIRCHES, BERNE, INDIANA 46711   WWW.WHITEBIRCHES.COM

Spring Blossoms

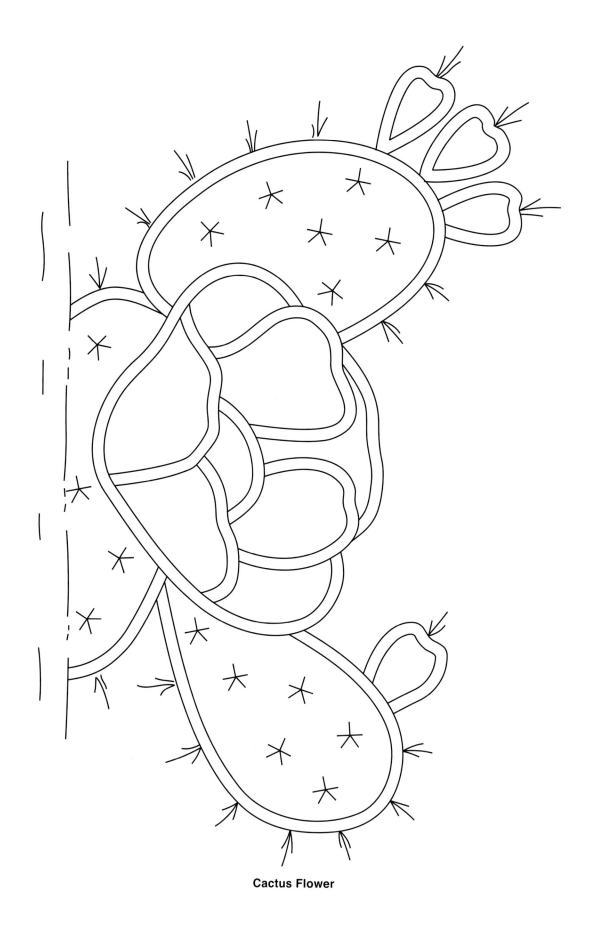

Cactus Flower

HOUSE OF WHITE BIRCHES, BERNE, INDIANA 46711   WWW.WHITEBIRCHES.COM

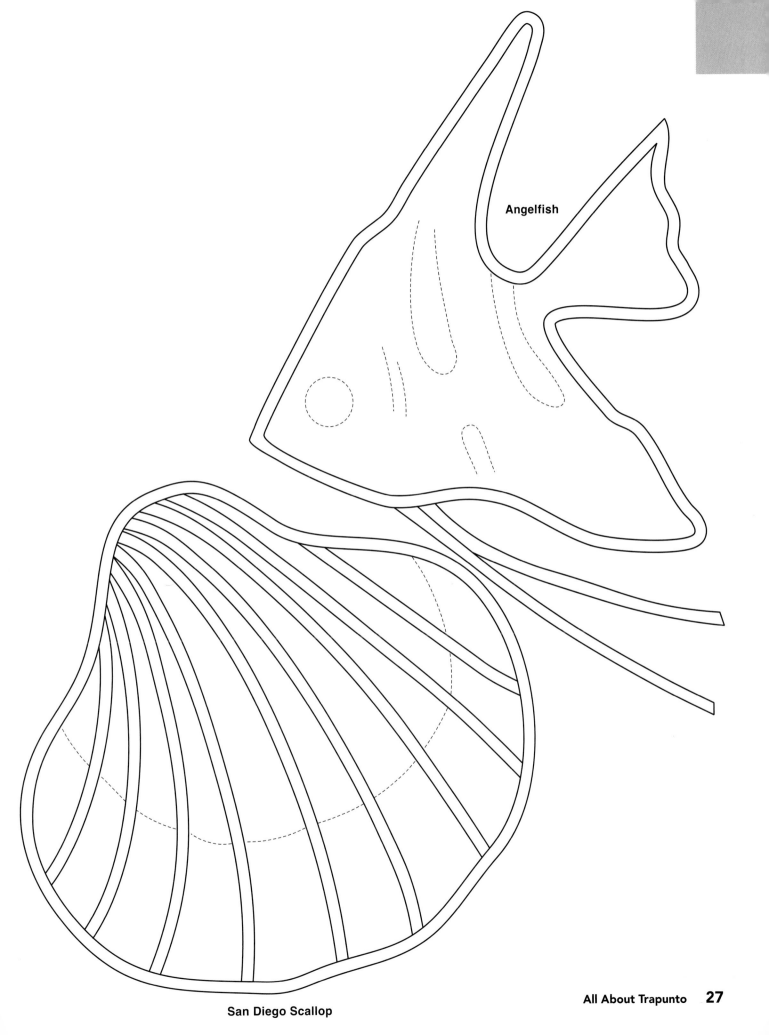

Angelfish

San Diego Scallop

Flying Jewels

Meadow Flower

HOUSE OF WHITE BIRCHES, BERNE, INDIANA 46711 WWW.WHITEBIRCHES.COM

Lighthouse

Striped Butterfly

Flower Cart

HOUSE OF WHITE BIRCHES, BERNE, INDIANA 46711 WWW.WHITEBIRCHES.COM

Jack Be Nimble

Sail Boat

HOUSE OF WHITE BIRCHES, BERNE, INDIANA 46711   WWW.WHITEBIRCHES.COM

Schooner

Spring Flowers
Dots denote possible beads or French knots.

HOUSE OF WHITE BIRCHES, BERNE, INDIANA 46711   WWW.WHITEBIRCHES.COM

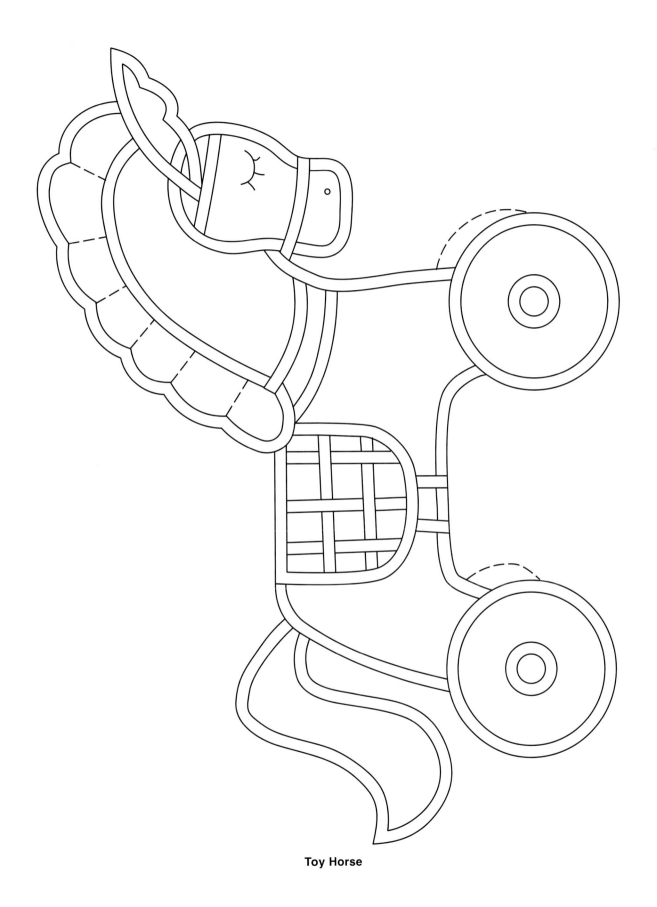

Toy Horse

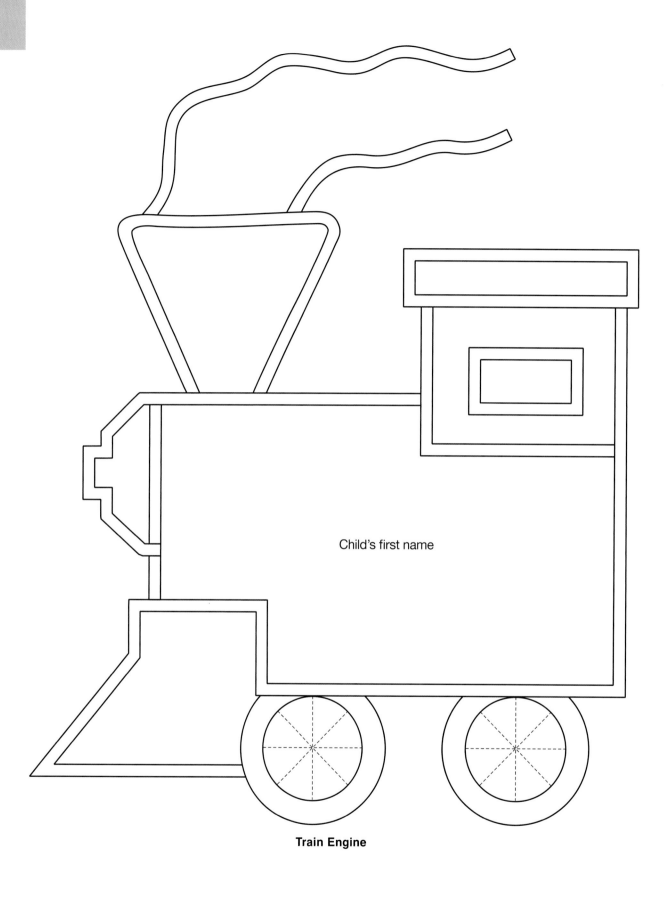

Child's first name

Train Engine

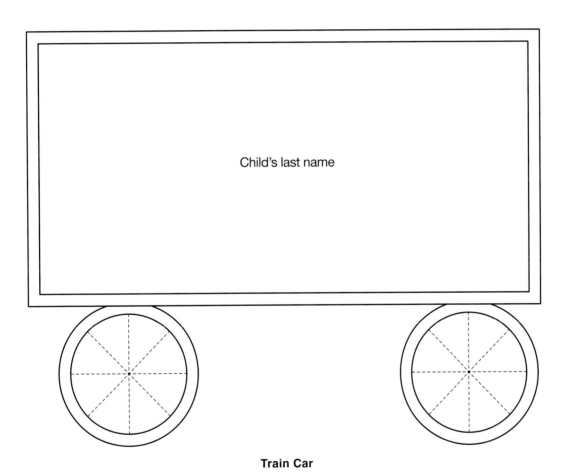

Child's last name

Train Car

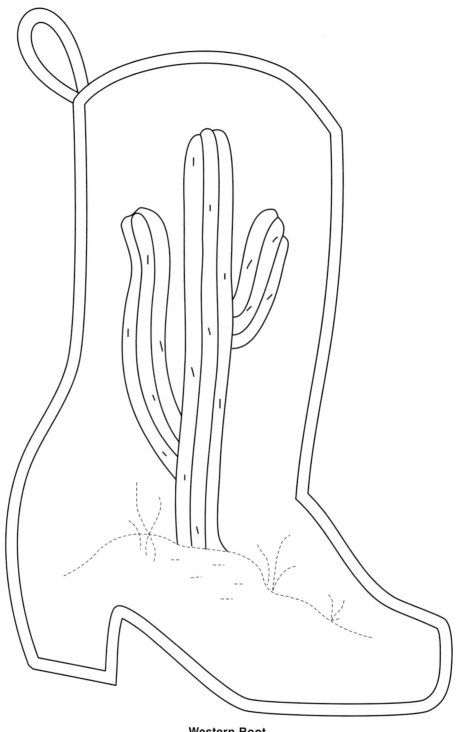

Western Boot

HOUSE OF WHITE BIRCHES, BERNE, INDIANA 46711   WWW.WHITEBIRCHES.COM

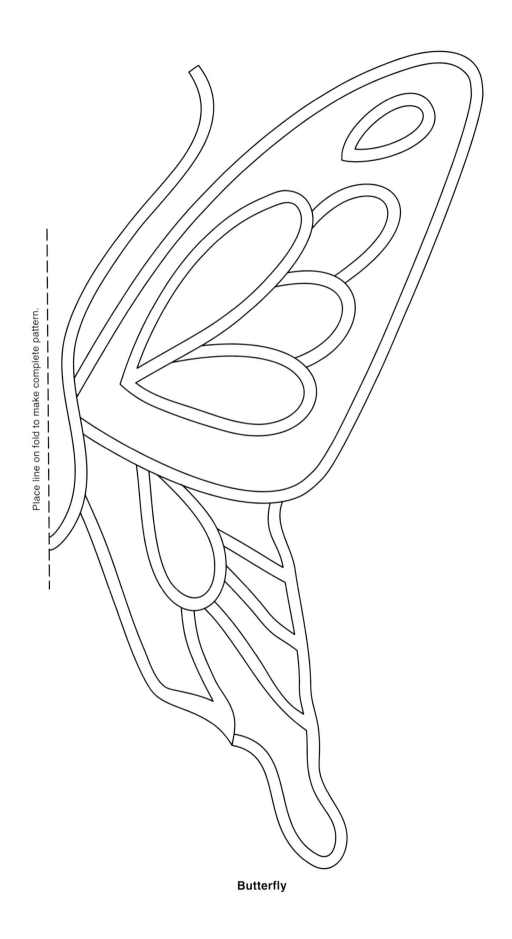

Place line on fold to make complete pattern.

Butterfly

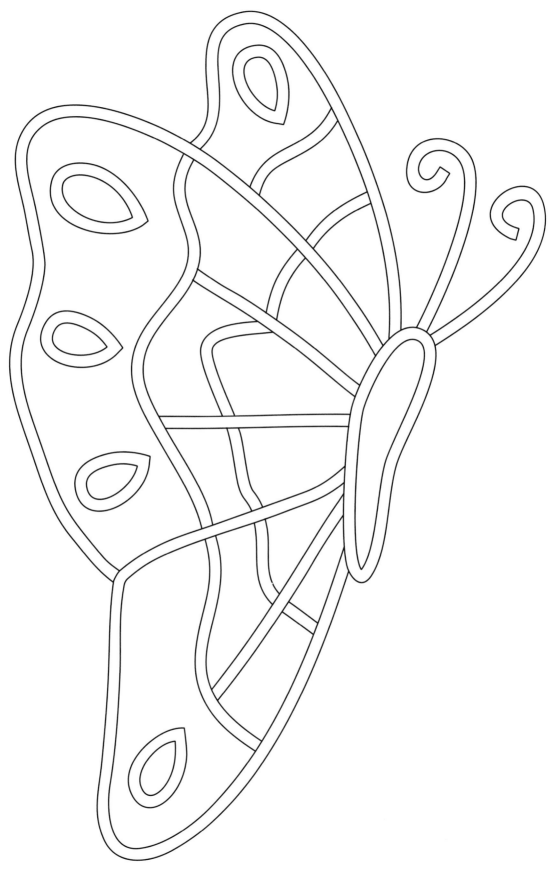

Butterfly in Flight

HOUSE OF WHITE BIRCHES, BERNE, INDIANA 46711   WWW.WHITEBIRCHES.COM

Butterfly in the Round

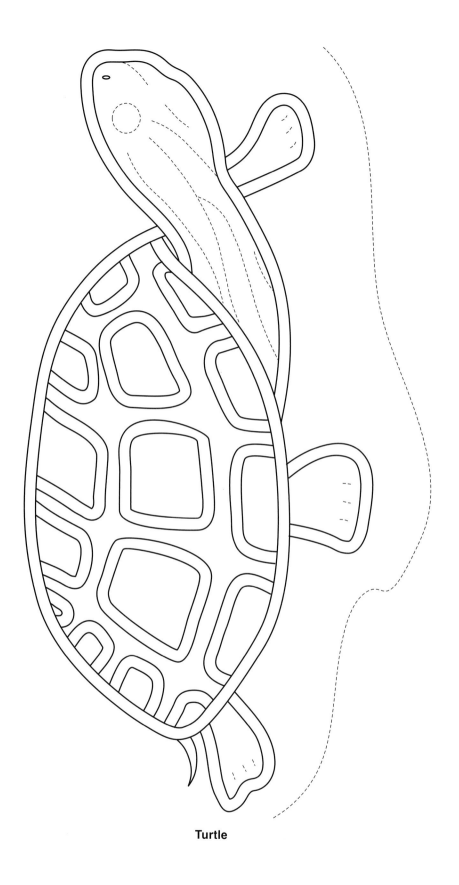

Turtle

HOUSE OF WHITE BIRCHES, BERNE, INDIANA 46711 WWW.WHITEBIRCHES.COM

Romantic Heart

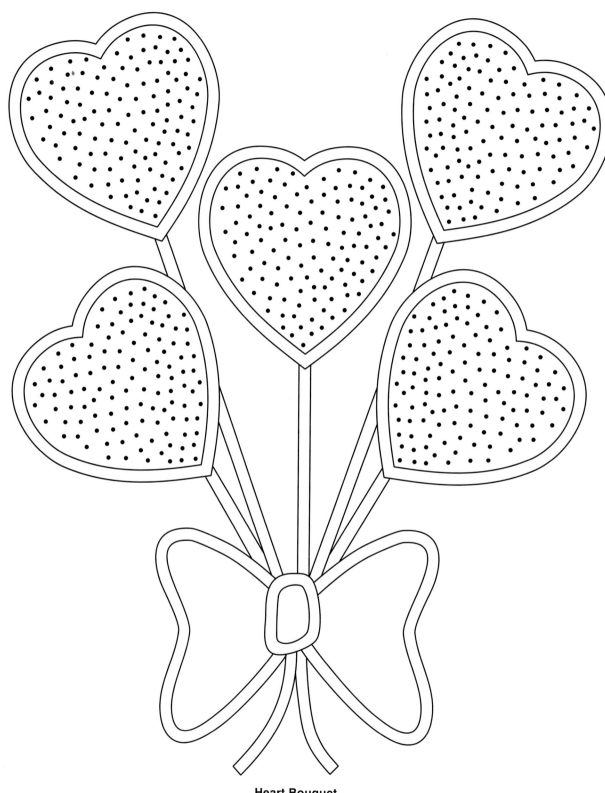

Heart Bouquet
Dots denote colonial knots or beads.

HOUSE OF WHITE BIRCHES, BERNE, INDIANA 46711   WWW.WHITEBIRCHES.COM

Place line on fold to make complete pattern.

Multiple Hearts

Place line on fold to make complete pattern.

Heart Medallion

Celtic Ring

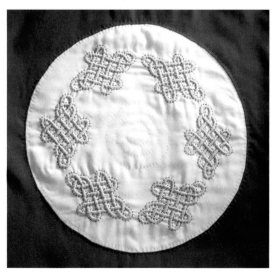

8" circle

HOUSE OF WHITE BIRCHES, BERNE, INDIANA 46711   WWW.WHITEBIRCHES.COM

Star in the Round

Time & Tide

HOUSE OF WHITE BIRCHES, BERNE, INDIANA 46711   WWW.WHITEBIRCHES.COM

Place line on fold to make complete pattern.

Intertwining Maze

Loop to Loop

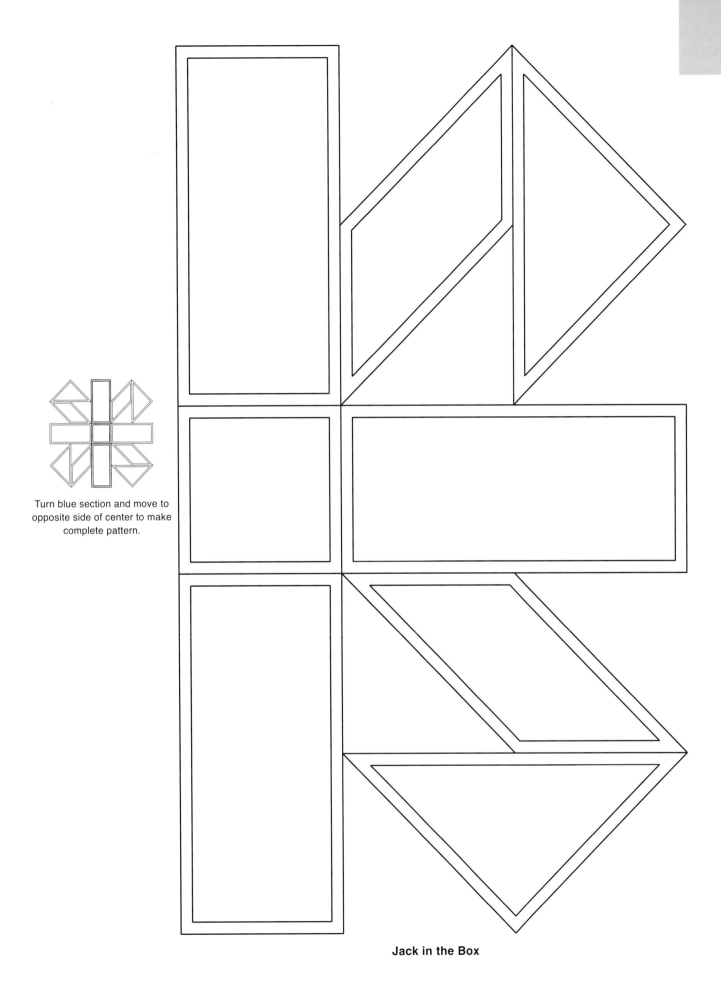

Turn blue section and move to opposite side of center to make complete pattern.

Jack in the Box

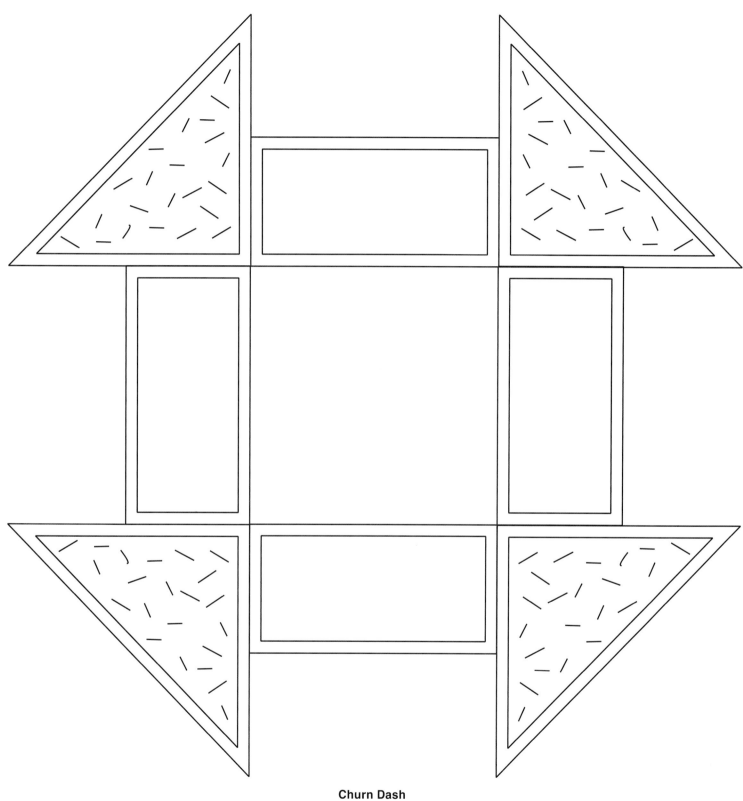

Churn Dash
Small lines denote possible seed stitches or French knots.

HOUSE OF WHITE BIRCHES, BERNE, INDIANA 46711   WWW.WHITEBIRCHES.COM

Ohio Star
Small lines denote possible seed stitches or French knots.

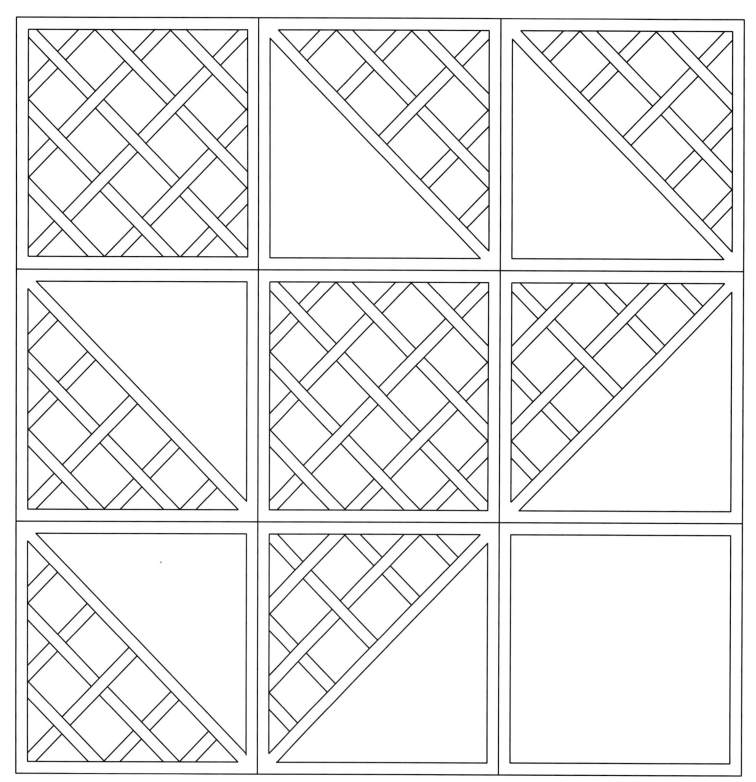

Sawtooth

Wings
Small lines denote possible seed stitches or French knots.

Place line on fold to make complete pattern.

Cathedral Window

HOUSE OF WHITE BIRCHES, BERNE, INDIANA 46711 WWW.WHITEBIRCHES.COM

Holiday Tree

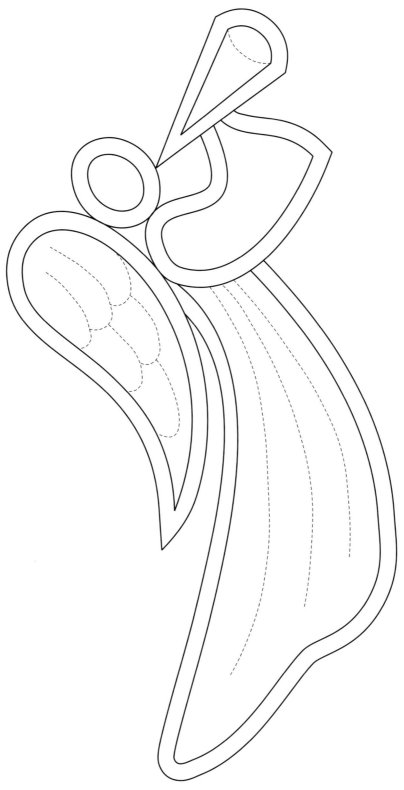

Angel With Trumpet

HOUSE OF WHITE BIRCHES, BERNE, INDIANA 46711 WWW.WHITEBIRCHES.COM

Stocking

Bells

Tree

HOUSE OF WHITE BIRCHES, BERNE, INDIANA 46711 WWW.WHITEBIRCHES.COM

Poinsettia

Letters

HOUSE OF WHITE BIRCHES, BERNE, INDIANA 46711 WWW.WHITEBIRCHES.COM

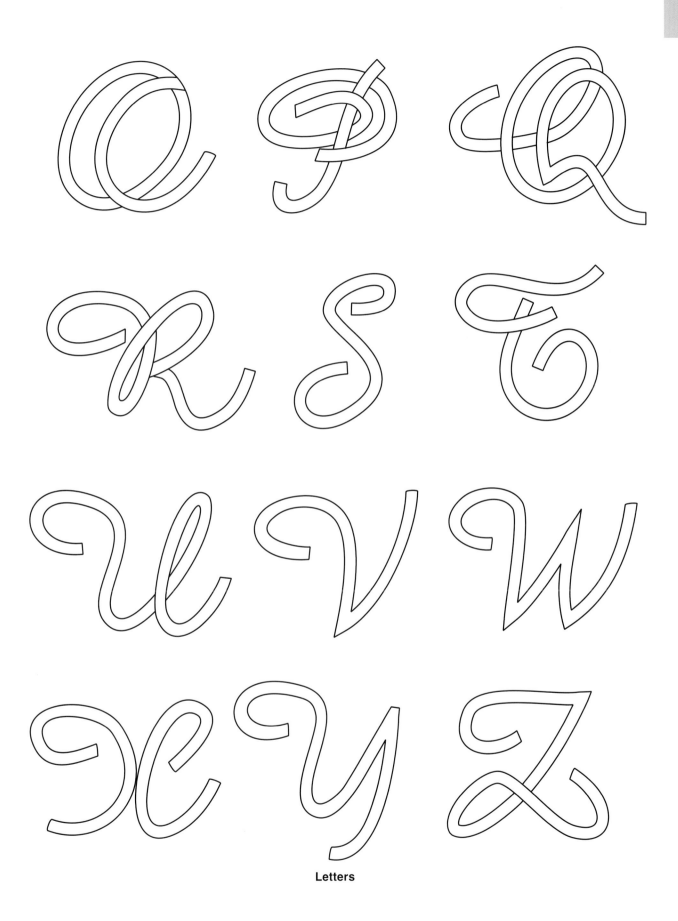

Letters

Numbers

E-mail: Customer_Service@whitebirches.com

All About Trapunto is published by House of White Birches, 306 East Parr Road, Berne, IN 46711, telephone (260) 589-4000. Printed in USA. Copyright © 2005 House of White Birches.

RETAILERS: If you would like to carry this pattern book or any other House of White Birches publications, call the Wholesale Department at Annie's Attic to set up a direct account: (903) 636-4303. Also, request a complete listing of publications available from House of White Birches.

Every effort has been made to ensure that the instructions in this pattern book are complete and accurate. We cannot, however, take responsibility for human error, typographical mistakes or variations in individual work.

ISBN: 1-59217-033-1
1 2 3 4 5 6 7 8 9

STAFF

Editors: Jeanne Stauffer, Sandra L. Hatch
Associate Editor: Dianne Schmidt
Technical Artist: Connie Rand
Copy Supervisor: Michelle Beck
Copy Editors: Nicki Lehman,
   Beverly Richardson
Graphic Arts Supervisor: Ronda Bechinski

Graphic Artists: Debby Keel,
   Edith Teegarden
Art Director: Brad Snow
Assistant Art Director: Nick Pierce
Photography: Christena Green
Photo Stylists: Tammy Nussbaum,
   Tammy M. Smith

Special thanks goes to Marsha Whittaker for her encouragement, proofreading and stitching of many of the samples.
The designer would also like to thank other friends/students for allowing her to include their work in the book.
Cover project stitched by Neva Pharr.

1071152605